To ————————————

From ————————————

A Little Spoonful of
Chicken Soup for the Soul®
A 2nd Helping

Published by Blessings Unlimited, Pentagon Towers
P.O. Box 398004, Edina, MN 55439

Photo by Willard Clay

Design by Lecy Design

ISBN 1-58375-543-8
Printed in Mexico

A
Little
Spoonful
of

Chicken
Soup
for the Soul
A 2nd Helping

Permission to Cry

Alone in the wheel of light at the dining room table, surrounded by an otherwise darkened house, I sat in tears. Finally, I'd succeeded in getting both kids to bed. A relatively new single parent, I had to be both Mommy and Daddy to my two little children. I got them both washed, accompanied by shrieks of delight, crazy running around, laughing and throwing things. More or less calmed down, they lay in their beds as I gave each the prescribed five minutes of back rubs. Then I took up my guitar and began the nighttime ritual of folk songs, ending with "All the Pretty Little Horses," both kids'

favorite. I sang it over and over, gradually reducing tempo and the volume until they seemed fully engaged in sleep.

A recently divorced man with full custody of his children, I was determined to give them as normal and stable home life as possible. I put on a happy face for them. I kept their activities as close to how they had always been as I could. This nightly ritual was just as it had always been with the exception that their mother was now missing. There, I had done it again: another night successfully concluded.

I had risen slowly, gingerly, trying to avoid

making even the least sound which might start them up again, asking for more songs and more stories. I tiptoed out of their room, closed the door part way, and went downstairs.

Sitting at the dining room table, I slumped in my chair, aware that this was the first time since I came home from work that I'd been able to sit down. I had cooked and served and encouraged two little ones to eat. I had done the dishes while responding to their many requests for attention. I helped my oldest with her second grade homework and appreciated my youngest's drawings and oohed over his elaborate construction of Lego blocks. The bath, the stories, the backrubs, the singing and now, at long last, a brief moment for myself. The silence was a relief, for the moment.

Then it all crowded in on me: the fatigue, the weight of the responsibility, the worry about bills I wasn't sure I could pay that month. The endless details of running a house. Only a short time before, I'd been married and had a partner to share these chores, these bills, these worries.

And the loneliness. I felt as though I were at the bottom of a great sea of loneliness. It all came together and I was at once lost, overwhelmed. Unexpected, convulsive sobs overtook me. I sat there, silently sobbing.

Just then, a pair of little arms went around my middle and a little face peered up at me. I looked down into my five-year-old son's sympathetic face.

I was embarrassed to be seen crying by my son. "I'm sorry, Ethan, I didn't know you were still awake." I don't know why it is, but so many people apologize when they cry and I was no exception. "I didn't mean to cry. I'm sorry. I'm just a little sad tonight."

"It's okay, Daddy. It's okay to cry, you're just a person."

I can't express how happy he made me, this little boy, who in the wisdom of innocence, gave me permission to cry. He seemed to be saying that I didn't have to always be strong, that it was occasionally possible to allow myself to feel weak and let out my feelings.

He crept into my lap and we hugged and talked for a while, and I took him back up to his bed and tucked him in. Somehow, it was possible for me to get to sleep that night, too. Thank you, my son.

Hanoch McCarty

A 4th Course of Chicken Soup for the Soul

You cannot teach

people anything.

You can only help

them discover it within themselves.

GALILEO

The Donor

My grown daughter, Sara, and I were very good friends. She lived with her family in a nearby town which allowed us to see each other very often. In between visits we wrote or talked on the phone.

When she called me, she always said, "Hi, Mom, it's me," and I'd say, "Hi, Me, how are you today?" She often signed her letters simply, "Me." Sometimes I'd call her "Me" just to tease.

Then my poor Sara died suddenly, without warning, from a brain hemorrhage. Needless to say, I was devastated! There can be no worse pain for a parent than to lose a beloved child. It took all my considerable faith to keep going.

We decided to donate her organs so at least that much good would come from an otherwise tragic situation. In due time, I heard from the Organ Retrieval Group telling me where all her organs went. No names were mentioned, of course.

About one year later, I received a beautiful letter from the young man who received her pancreas and kidney. What a difference it made in his life!

Praise God! And since he couldn't use his

own name, guess how he signed his letter: "Me!"

My cup runneth over.

Mary M. Jelinek

A 4th Course of Chicken Soup for the Soul

A Final Goodbye

"I am going home to Denmark, Son, and I just wanted to tell you I love you."

In my dad's last telephone call to me, he repeated that line several times in a half hour. I wasn't listening at the right level. I heard his words, but not the message, and certainly not their profound intent. I believed my dad would live to be over 100 years old, as my great-uncle lived to be 107 years old. I had not felt his remorse over Mom's death, understood his intense loneliness as an "empty nester," or realized most of his pals had long since light-beamed off the planet. He relentlessly requested my brothers and I create grandchildren so that he could be a devoted grandfather. I was too busy "enterpreneuring" to really listen.

"Dad's dead," sighed my brother Brian on July 4, 1973.

My little brother is a witty lawyer and has a humorous, quick mind. I thought he was setting me up for a joke, and I awaited the punchline...there wasn't one. "Dad died in the bed he was born in...in Rozkeldj," continued Brian. "The funeral directors are putting him in a coffin, and shipping Dad and his belongings to us by tomorrow. We need to prepare for the funeral."

I was speechless. This isn't the way it's supposed to happen. If I knew these were to be Dad's final days, I would have asked to go with him to Denmark. I believe in the hospice movement, which says: "No one should die alone." A loved one should hold your hand and comfort you as you transition from one plane of reality to another. I would have offered consolation during his final hour, if I'd been really listening, thinking and in tune with the Infinite. Dad announced his departure as best he could, and I had missed it. I felt grief, pain and remorse. Why had I not been there for him? He's always been there for me.

In the mornings when I was nine years old, he would come home from working 18 hours at his bakery and wake me up at 5:00 A.M. by scratching my back with his strong, powerful hands and whispering, "Time to get up, Son." By the time I was dressed and ready to roll, he had my newspapers folded, banded and stuffed in my bicycle basket. Recalling his generosity of spirit brings tears to my eyes.

When I was racing bicycles, he drove me 50 miles each way to Kenosha, Wisconsin, every Tuesday night so I could race and he could watch me. He was there to hold me if I lost and shared the euphoria when I won.

Later, he accompanied me to all my local talks in Chicago when I spoke to Century 21, Mary Kay, Equitable and various churches. He always smiled, listened and proudly told whomever he was sitting with, "That's my boy!"

After the fact, my heart was in pain because Dad was there for me and I wasn't there for him. My humble advice is to always, always share your love with your loved ones, and ask to be invited to that sacred transitional period where physical life transforms into spiritual life. Experiencing the process of death with one you love will take

you into a bigger, more expansive dimension
of beingness.

Mark Victor Hansen

A 2nd Helping of Chicken Soup for the Soul

The marvelous richness of human experience would lose something of rewarding joy if there were no limitations to overcome. The hilltop hour would not be half so wonderful if there were no dark valleys to traverse.

HELEN KELLER

The Only Memory That Lingers

I have many memories about my father and about growing up with him in our apartment next to the elevated train tracks. For 20 years, we listened to the roar of the train as it passed by his bedroom window. Late at night, he waited alone on the tracks for the train that took him to his job at a factory, where he worked the midnight shift.

On this particular night, I waited with him in the dark to say good-bye. His face was grim. His youngest son had been drafted. I would be sworn in at six the next morning, while he stood at his paper-cutting machine in the factory.

My father had talked about his anger. He didn't want them to take his child, only 19 years old, who had never had a drink or smoked a cigarette, to fight a war in Europe. He placed his hands on my slim shoulders. "You be careful, Srulic, and if you ever need anything, write to me and I'll see that you get it."

Suddenly, he heard the roar of the approaching train. He held me tightly in his arms and gently kissed me on the cheek. With tear-filled eyes, he murmured, "I love you, my son." Then the train arrived, the doors closed him inside, and he disappeared into the night.

One month later, at age 46, my father died. I am 76 as I sit and write this. I once heard Pete Hamill, the New York reporter, say that memories are man's greatest inheritance, and I have to agree. I've lived through four invasions in World War II. I've had a life full of all kinds of experiences. But the only memory that lingers is of the night when my dad said, "I love you, my son."

TED KRUGER

A 4th Course of Chicken Soup for the Soul

Do not look back in anger;
or forward in fear, but around
in awareness.

JAMES THURBER

I'm not afraid of storms,

for I'm learning how to

sail my ship.

LOUISA MAY ALCOTT

The Lesson Plan

It was just an ordinary day. The children came to school on buses; there was the usual hubbub of excitement as they greeted each other. I looked over my plan book and I never felt better prepared to face the day. It would be a good day, I knew, and we would accomplish a lot. We took our places around the reading table and settled in for a good reading class. The first thing on my agenda was to check workbooks to see that the necessary work had been completed.

When I came to Troy, he had his head down as he shoved his unfinished assignment in front of me. He tried to pull himself back out of my sight as he sat on my right-hand side. Naturally, I looked at the incomplete work and said, "Troy, this is not finished."

He looked up at me with the most pleading eyes I have seen in a child and said, "I couldn't do it last night 'cuz my mother is dying."

The sobs that followed startled the entire class. How glad I was that he was sitting next to me. Yes, I took him in my arms and his head rested against my chest. There was no doubt in anyone's mind that Troy was hurting, hurting so much that I was afraid his little heart would break. His sobs echoed through the room and tears flowed copiously. The children sat with tear-filled eyes in dead silence. Only Troy's sobs broke the stillness of that morning class. One child raced for the Kleenex box while I just pressed his little body closer to my heart. I could feel my blouse being soaked by those precious tears. Helplessly, my tears fell upon his head.

The question that confronted me was, "What do I do for a child who is losing his mother?" The only thought that came to my mind was, "Love him...show him you care...cry with him." It seemed as though the whole bottom was coming out of his young life, and I could do little to help him. Choking back my tears, I said to the group, "Let us say a prayer for Troy and his mother." A more fervent prayer never floated to heaven. After some time, Troy looked up at me and said, "I think I will be okay now." He had exhausted his supply of tears; he released the burden of his heart. Later that afternoon, Troy's mother died.

When I went to the funeral parlor, Troy rushed to greet me. It was as though he had been waiting for me, that he expected I would come. He fell into my arms and just rested there awhile. He seemed to gain strength and courage, and then he led me to the coffin. There he was able to look into the face of his mother, to face death even though he might never be able to understand the mystery of it.

That night I went to bed thanking God that he had given me the good sense to set aside my reading plan and to hold the broken heart of a child in my own heart.

SISTER CARLEEN BRENNAN

A 4th Course of Chicken Soup for the Soul

The worst prison would be a

closed heart.

POPE JOHN PAUL II

A happy person is not a person in a certain set of circumstances, but rather a person with a certain set of attitudes.

HUGH DOWNS

Looking Down

Up there you go around every hour and a half; time after time, after time, and you wake up in the morning over the Mid-East, and over North Africa. You look out of your window as you're eating breakfast—and there's the whole Mediterranean area, and Greece and Rome, and the Sinai and Israel. And you realize that what you are seeing in one glance was the whole history of man for centuries; the cradle of civilization.

You go across the Atlantic Ocean, back across North Africa. You do it again and again. You identify with Houston, and then you identify with Los Angeles, and Phoenix and New Orleans. And the next thing you know, you are starting to identify with North Africa. You look forward to it. You anticipate it. And the whole process of what you identify with begins to shift.

When you go around it every hour and a half, you begin to recognize that your identity is with that whole thing. And that makes a very powerful change inside of you....

As you look down you can't imagine how many borders and boundaries you cross—again and again. And you can't even see them. But you know that in the "wake-up" scene you saw before over the Mid-East, there are thousands of people fighting over some imaginary line that you can't even see. And you wish you could take each of them hand in hand, and say, "Look at that! Look at that! What's important?"

Later the person sitting next to you goes out to the moon. And he sees the earth, not as something big with all kinds of beautiful details; he sees it as a small thing out there. And the contrast between that small blue and white Christmas tree ornament and that black sky really comes through…and you realize that on that little blue and white spot is everything that means anything to you—

all history, and music, and war, and death, and birth, and love, and tears, and joy—all of it on that little blue and white spot that you can cover with your thumb.

It comes through to you so clearly that you are a sensing point for man. You look down and you see the surface of the glove that you have lived on all this time and you know that all those people down there—they are you. And somehow, you represent them and have a responsibility to them. Somehow you recognize that you are a piece of this total life. You're out there on the forefront and you have to bring your experience back somehow.

It becomes a rather special responsibility, and it tells you about your relationship to this thing we call the world.

And through this I've used the word "you" because it's not me, Rusty Schweickart...or any of the others that have had this experience. It's not just my problem—my challenge—my job to integrate into daily life. It's everyone's.

RUSTY SCHWEICKART

A 4th Course of Chicken Soup for the Soul

Three things in human

life are important:

The first is to be kind.

The second is to be kind.

The third is to be kind.

HENRY JAMES

―――――――――――――――――

Spread love everywhere you go:
First of all in your own house…let no one
ever come to you without leaving better and
happier. Be the living expression of God's
kindness; kindness in your face, kindness
in your eyes, kindness in your smile,
kindness in your warm greeting.

MOTHER TERESA

―――――――――――――――――

Attitude...One of
Life's Choices

My wife, Tere, and I purchased a new car in December. Even though we had tickets to fly from California to Houston to visit her family for Christmas, we decided to drive to Texas to break in the new car. We packed the car and took off for a wonderful week with Grandma.

We had a wonderful time and stayed to the last possible minute visiting with Grandma. On the return trip we needed to get home in a hurry, so we drove straight through—one person driving while the other one slept. After driving in a hard rain for several hours, we arrived home late at night. We were tired and ready for a hot shower and a soft bed. I had the feeling that no matter how tired we were, we should unpack the car that night, but all Tere wanted was the hot shower and the soft bed, so we decided to wait and unload the car in the morning.

At seven o'clock in the morning, we got up refreshed and ready to unpack the car. When we opened the front door, there was no car in the driveway! Tere and I looked at each other, looked back at the driveway, looked at each other, looked back at the driveway, and looked at each other again. Then Tere asked this wonderful question, "Well, where did you park the car?"

Laughing, I answered, "Right in the driveway." Now we knew where we had parked the car, but we still walked outside, hoping that maybe the car had miraculously backed out the driveway and parked itself by the curb, but it hadn't.

Stunned, we called the police and filed a report that supposedly activated our high-tech tracking system. To be on the safe side, I also called the tracking system company. They assured me they had a 98 percent recovery rate within two hours. In two hours, I called again and asked, "Where's my car?"

"We haven't found it yet, Mr. Harris, but we have a 94 percent recovery rate within four hours."

Two more hours passed. I called again and asked, "Where's my car?"

Again they answered, "We haven't found it yet, but we have a 90 percent recovery rate of finding it within eight hours."

At that point I told them, "Your percentage rate means nothing to me when I'm in the small percentage, so call me when you find it."

Later that day, a commercial aired on television with the automaker asking, "Wouldn't you like to have this car in your driveway?"

I responded, "Sure I would! I had one yesterday."

As the day unfolded, Tere became increasingly upset as she remembered more and more of what had been in the car—our wedding album, irreplaceable family photos from past generations, clothes, all of our camera equipment, my wallet and our checkbooks, just to name a few. These were items of little importance to our survival, yet they seemed of major importance at that moment.

Anxious and frustrated, Tere asked me,

"How can you joke about this when all of these things and our brand new car are missing?"

I looked at her and said, "Honey, we can have a stolen car and be all upset, or we can have a stolen car and be happy. Either way, we have a stolen car. I truly believe our attitudes and moods are our choice and right now I choose to be happy."

Five days later our car was returned without a trace of any of our belongings, and with over $3,000 worth of damage to the car. I took it to the dealer for repair and was happy to hear they would have it back to us within a week.

At the end of that week, I dropped off the rental and picked up our car. I was excited and relieved to have our own car back. Unfortunately, these feelings were short-lived. On the way home, I rear-ended another car right at our freeway exit ramp. It didn't hurt the car I ran into, but it sure hurt ours — another $3,000 worth of damage and another insurance claim. I managed to drive the car into our driveway, but when I got out to survey the damage, the left front tire went flat.

As I was standing in the driveway looking at the car, kicking myself in the tail for hitting the other car, Tere arrived home. She walked up to me, looked at the car, and then at me. Seeing I was beating myself up, she put her arm around me and said, "Honey, we can have a wrecked car and be all upset, or we can have a wrecked car and be happy. Either way, we have a wrecked car, so let's choose to be happy."

I surrendered with a hearty laugh and we went on to have a wonderful evening together.

BOB HARRIS

A 2nd Helping of Chicken Soup for the Soul

We cannot live only for ourselves.

A thousand fibers connect us

with our fellow men!

HERMAN MELVILLE

I'll Do
Anything!

Jack had cerebral palsy. He was quadriplegic and used the restricted motion he had in one hand to push the lever that propelled his electric wheelchair. Although he was not one of my students, he often listened to my lectures and participated in discussion groups. I had a difficult time understanding his speech and relied heavily on classmates to interpret for him. He shared his personal concerns and frustrations with me, deeply touching my heart. He was so courageous to be so vulnerable!

One day after class, Jack came up to me and said he wanted to work. At the time I was training severely disabled adults to work at on- and off-campus jobs at Fresno City College. I asked Jack, "Where?"

He said, "With you in the cafeteria." Stunned for a moment, I thought about the skills needed to perform the tasks of bussing tables, loading dishwashers, sweeping, mopping, stocking, etc. How could a person who is quadriplegic possible participate in this type of training program? I couldn't answer. My mind was blank.

"What do you want to do Jack?" I asked, hoping he might have something in mind.

His response was firm. "I'll do anything!"

he said with a smile. Oh, how I loved his spirit and determination and admired his conviction! We made arrangements to meet in the cafeteria at 10:00 A.M. the following day. I wondered if he would be punctual. Could he even tell time? The next morning I heard his wheelchair 15 minutes early for his appointment. I silently prayed for guidance and insight.

At 10:00 A.M., we met. By 10:01, Jack was ready to go to work. His enthusiasm made his speech even more difficult to understand. In my endeavors to find a way for Jack to participate meaningfully in a vocational training program, I ran into one obstacle after another. His wheel chair kept him from getting too close to tables. He was unable to use his hands except to grasp. I tried some adaptations without success. Seeing my frustration, a kind-hearted custodian offered to help. Within a half hour, he had provided a solution. He had shortened the handle of a floor mop so it fit comfortably under Jack's arm and could be manipulated with one hand. The mop was positioned to reach the table tops. With the other hand, Jack propelled his chair, wiping the surface of the tables as he moved around.

Jack was in heaven! He was so proud to be an active participant and not just an observer! As I watched, I noticed that he could push chairs out of the way using his wheelchair. A new job was created for Jack: pushing chairs away from tables that were designated for wheelchair use and lining them up against the wall out of the way. Jack performed his job with gusto and pride. His self-esteem soared! At last, he felt capable and worthwhile!

One day Jack came to me in tears. When I asked what was wrong, he explained to me that people were not letting him do his job.

At first I didn't understand what he meant. Then I observed him trying to move chairs. It took so much effort on his part that well-intentioned students thought he was struggling to get chairs out of his way and they would move the chairs for him. He tried to explain, but no one took the time to listen. The problem was solved when I made these cards for Jack to carry on his tray:

Hi! My name is Jack. I am working in the cafeteria. My job is to wipe down tables and move certain chairs to the wall. If you would like to help me, PLEASE give me a big smile and tell me what a good job I am doing.

Jack displayed and shared these cards proudly. Students began taking Jack and his job seriously. That semester, he experienced the self-worth that comes when one feels acknowledged and supported. His determination will always be an inspiration to me, as I search for and find new ways for my students and I to overcome life's obstacles and be all we can with our God-given talents.

DOLLY TROUT
A 4th Course of Chicken Soup for the Soul

Keep away from people who try to belittle
your ambitions. Small people always do that,
but the really great make you feel that you,
too, can become great.

MARK TWAIN